TONIGHT, JOSEPHINE
and other undiscovered letters

Other books by Michael Green

The Coarse series
The Art of Coarse Rugby
The Art of Coarse Sailing
Even Coarser Rugby
The Art of Coarse Sport
The Art of Coarse Acting
The Art of Coarse Golf
The Art of Coarse Moving (A Roof Over My Head)
The Art of Coarse Drinking
The Art of Coarse Cruising
Even Coarser Sport
The Art of Coarse Sex

Novels
Don't Print My Name Upside Down
Squire Haggard's Journal

Plays
Four Plays for Coarse Actors (The Coarse Acting Show)
The Coarse Acting Show 2

Others
Michael Green's Rugby Alphabet
Stage Noises and Effects

Tonight Josephine

AND OTHER UNDISCOVERED LETTERS

by MICHAEL GREEN
author of THE ART of COARSE books

Drawings by JOHN JENSEN

SECKER & WARBURG
LONDON

First published in England 1981 by
Martin Secker & Warburg Limited
54 Poland Street, London W1V 3DF

ISBN: 0-436-18793 0

Printed and bound in Great Britain by
Morrison & Gibb Ltd, London and Edinburgh

FOREWORD

Just a word of thanks for friends who put forward
suggestions for this book, especially Peter Grose,
Richard Gaunt, Wilfred Sharp and Geoff Webb
(who has lost most of his friends since I mentioned
him in *The Art of Coarse Sex*). Also to Frank di
Rienzo, proprietor of the Venezia Restaurant, Soho,
where a great deal of this volume was written on
the tablecloth.

Michael Green
London, 1981

From: Napoleon Bonaparte, Emperor
of the French; First Consul for
Life; First Citizen of France; King
in absentia of the United Kingdom
of Great Britain and Ireland;
Commander-in-Chief of the Imperial
Grand Army of France; Commander
of the First Military District;
Commander of the Second Military
District; Commander of the Third
Military District; Colonel-in-Chief
of the Old Guard; Head of the
Deuxième Bureau; Controller of the
Troisième Bureau; Commander of
the Légion d'Honneur; Chief of the
Imperial Order of St. Anthony;
holder of the Médaille Militaire with
oak leaves; holder of the award for
meritorious service (with branches).

To: The Empress Josephine of all
France; Queen *in absentia* of the
United Kingdom of Great Britain
and Ireland; Grand Dame of the
Imperial Order of St. Anthony.

Tilsit, Saturday

Tonight, Josephine

Boney

From: The Empress Josephine of all France, Queen *in absentia* of the United Kingdom and Ireland; Grand Dame of the Imperial Order of St. Anthony.

To: Napoleon Bonaparte, Emperor of the French; First Consul for Life; First Citizen of France; King *in absentia* of the United Kingdom of Great Britain and Ireland; Commander-in-Chief of the Imperial Grand Army of France; Commander of the First Military District; Commander of the Second Military District; Commander of the Third Military District; Colonel-in-Chief of the Old Guard; Head of the Deuxième Bureau; Controller of the Troisième Bureau; Commander of the Légion d'Honneur; Chief of the Imperial Order of St. Anthony; holder of the Médaille Militaire with oak leaves; holder of the award for meritorious service (with branches).

Sorry, headache.

Josephine

Dear Mr. Wright,

When are you going to finish repairing my bicycle? It is six months since I gave it to you and you have still not returned it. In my opinion you and your brother Wilbur spend too much time on those flying machines of yours. You would do better to pay more attention to your customers.

Another thing: I watched one of your machines the other day and the wheels looked just like they had come right off my bicycle. You had no right to take them like that without asking. Also, as you get higher the air gets thinner and the tyres will explode. That is assuming you bothered to mend the punctures. I guess the thing the driver was steering by also looked mighty like my handlebars.

Then there is Widow Hutchinson. She says you promised to tune her piano and you've not returned it. She believes you are using the wire to hold those goddam machines together. You may deny it, but I tell you when one of them crashed the other afternoon it sounded like someone playing The Lost Chord at Carnegie Hall. I think that it is a dirty trick to play on an honest woman, or a dishonest one for that matter, and her only widowed three months.

You and your brother are a disgrace to the town of Kittyhawk.

Yours faithfully,

Abe Young

4

Dear Adolf,

I am writing as your ever-loving mother to ask you to give up these stupid politics and come home and settle down. What has got into you, rioting and getting into trouble with the police? You used to be such a quiet lad, happy with your painting and your biology experiments. You would spend hours pulling the legs off beetles. I believe the trouble is that you have got into the wrong set. I do not like the people you are mixing with, especially the fat one. He may have been in the air force during the war but that is no excuse for his drunken behaviour. And then there is that little cripple, the one you brought home who tried to rape Frau Bernstein. If he had not been club-footed, so she could run faster, he would have caught her and anything could have happened. Himmel, how he talked. Why does he hate everyone?

If you would only stick to your painting you could make a name for yourself. Remember how Frau Schmidt next door paid you three pfennigs for a portrait of her cat? All right, so you painted in five legs. Anyone can make a mistake. From little beginnings you could build up. You have already made a start. You don't want to be a nobody all your life, do you?

Your loving mother

P.S. Please shave off that silly moustache.

The Headmaster's House,
The Close,
Rugby School,
Warwickshire
July 2, 1840

Dear Mr. Brown,

I deeply regret that I have to ask you to take your son away from Rugby School immediately. Indeed, by the time you receive this letter he should already be on the mail coach to London.

I am afraid Brown has become a disturbing influence in the school. I need hardly tell you he is a good-looking youth with fair hair and an engaging manner. Alas, these good looks are coupled with a propensity for that unmentionable vice which caused the destruction of Sodom and Gomorrah and lest the town of Rugby suffer the same fate as those unhappiest of cities, we must root out every manifestation of this fearful practice.

In fairness to your son, he is less the perpetrator of this terrible vice than the recipient. The entire Sixth Form have fallen deeply in love with him. One unfortunate youth named Flashman, an older boy of somewhat weak character but of hitherto unblemished record, was so overcome by your son's charms that when thrown over he drank himself into insensibility through despised love. I had no choice but to expel him from the school for drunkenness, although I feel your son's flirtatiousness was largely to blame. I am reliably informed that there was a certain amount of sadism in the relationship between Brown and Flashman, including ceremonies of burning and flagellation. I may say that the expulsion of the unhappy Flashman was the first time I had sent a boy away since 1823, when that wretched youth William Webb Ellis was expelled for persistently cheating on the football field.

But *Vade retro satane* as the Romans would say. The whole is greater than the part. If thine eye offend thee, pluck it out, the Good Book advises us and while we shall miss your son, who showed great promise at cross-country running, we have to consider the good of the school as a whole. We cannot have a sink of iniquity festering in the Lower Fourth.

Mention of cross-country running reminds me that in our last Hare and Hounds event, your son was unfortunately cast in the role of Hare and was pursued through the countryside by the entire Sixth Form with such unprecedented vigour that the race only lasted twenty minutes, the shortest time on record. Alas, when the Sixth Form caught up with Brown there was an unseemly brawl as they fought over the right to possess the Hare and three runners had to be taken to the Infirmary. Brooke, the School Captain, informs me that on another occasion your son was the prize in the Upper School lottery.

If I may offer a word of advice, I hope Brown will not neglect his football, although it might be advisable for him not to play in the scrum. As regards his future, perhaps some artistic career might yet offer an opportunity for him to make a name for himself. Much may be achieved by prayer and fasting.

> I have the honour to be,
> sir
> Your obedient servant,
>
> Arnold

TX186 GLB0029 MEA001

GLBB CO MEME 016

REFORMA MEXICO DF MEX 16 10 1110

JAMES GORDON BENNETT TRIBNEWS

LONDON INGLATERRA

HAVE SEARCHED SOUTH AMERICA WITHOUT SUCCESS STOP

PLEASE ADVISE

      STANLEY

SENT 2256/10 CNL

OSEAGRAM 05 LN

262009 IHTLON G

Sign of the Vulture,
St. Paul's Churchyard,
London
Nov. 1, 1678

Dear Mr. Bunyan,

Many thanks for letting me see the manuscript of *Pilgrim's Progress*, which I am returning as I am afraid we cannot envisage a use for it in the foreseeable future. The fact is, there really isn't much demand for travel books at this moment in time. Also it is a bit gloomy in places.

Are you interested in madrigals, at all? We find there is a growing demand for books of this nature. We would also be quite interested in something based on your prison experiences.

Incidentally, I am afraid we have had to put *Grace Abounding to the Chief of Sinners* on the remainder list. It didn't do as well as expected. Perhaps it is unfortunate that it came out at the same time as *Paradise Lost*.

Yours sincerely,

Thos. Jarvis
Printer and bookbinder

Dear Mr. Wagner,

As you may know I often collaborate with Arthur Sullivan in the writing of comic operas which have been performed with some success in England in recent years. Unfortunately, Sullivan is a man of uncertain temperament, and has refused to write the score of my next opera on the grounds that he is going to be engaged for the next three years on a vast oratorio (he does have ambitions to make a name in serious music). I am therefore enquiring if you would like to undertake the task?

I enclose a copy of the first draft. As you will see, the plot concerns a group of pirates at Penzance, a fishing port in Cornwall, England, one of whose number, named Frederick, leaves them and falls in love with the beautiful daughter of a major-general. Various complications ensue which you will see from the manuscript, but in the end all are reunited and everything ends happily. I particularly draw your attention to the chorus of comic policemen in the second half of the piece, which should give great opportunities for the exercise of your musical genius, knowing your talent and skill in choral work.

Perhaps you would be kind enough to read the draft and give me your opinion. I might add I am a great fan of your work. I often hum *The Ride of the Valkyries* in the bath.

Yours sincerely,

W. S. Gilbert

Dear Mr. Gilbert,

   I am thanking you for your letter and the
manuscript which I enjoyed very much. My wife
Cosima says I have not laughed so much since her
father died. Yes, I believe I could undertake the task
of writing a score but first let me offer some
suggestions.

   I take it that Frederick, the central figure,
represents the eternal Wanderer or *Vogelgeist* and
that the daughters of the Major General are Sea
Maidens or *Wasserleitung*. This I shall explain with a
short song by Frederick in the first Act, *Himmel, Wo
Ist Mein Doppelganger?* This will take up most of Act
One, about three-quarters of an hour, and then the
Wasserleitung appear and render a spirited chorus of
Du Bist Ein Klott. But do not fear—I shall not
neglect the humour in this part. As Frederick is
singing, an old woman (Mathilde) appears in the
background and tries to climb up the cliff. We shall
have much mirth watching her pitiful efforts to
climb the rocks and then just when we think she has
succeeded she falls off the top and is killed! When I
read this idea to Cosima she could not stop laughing.

   Now for the pirates. I think it would be better if
they were all dwarfs (*Nibelung*), symbolising the
underworld. They should wear gnome's hats and
have long beards down to their waists as then the
audience will know they are dwarfs. They will
naturally sing a merry chorus every time they
appear:

Ho ho ho ho ho ho ho ho!
Curses on everybody.
Ho ho ho ho ho ho ho ho!
Curses on everybody.

(I have given the English version as the German is a little difficulty.)

And so we come to the policemen. I am afraid that here, Mr. Gilbert, I am finding myself in slight disagreement with you. It is most important that these jovial fellows have a mirth-making chorus but I find your version rather sad. It is not very merry, is it not, to suggest the life of a policeman is not a happy one? I would suggest instead a new chorus for the police, viz.: *Leb' wohl, leb' wohl, leb' wohl, hier ist das Krankenhaus*. This will make much mirth.

However, the climax of the opera, which is the clash between the pirates and the policemen, is a magnificent piece of writing, symbolising the eternal struggle between the forces of Evil Dominant, represented by the pirates, and Right Triumphant, represented by the police. Would it not, incidentally, be better if the police were giants? I am merely making the suggestion. But let us not be too serious, Mr. Gilbert. I would suggest that the pirates gain their victory over the police by putting out their eyes with tiny arrows! I can almost see you laughing at this idea. Thus it appears that Evil has triumphed, but then the Gods cause an earthquake in which all the dwarfs are killed (that is because being so small they slip down the cracks in the earth—I have thought out the details you see) and the opera ends with Frederick and the *Wasserleitung* singing *Donner Und Blitzen, Mein Vater Ist Ein Feuerwerk* while the maiden's father, the Major-General, commits self-immolation (Purification by Fire).

This I think will be a most amusing opera and if you like I will add some risible jokes to the libretto.

With best wishes,
Yours sincerely,

R. Wagner

Hampstead
Friday

My Dear Sullivan,
    Please forgive me for those harsh words the other
night. For various reasons which I will not go into, I
implore you to return to our partnership on any
terms you want to lay down.

                    Yours sincerely,

                    W. S. Gilbert

299858 PO WD G
299992 PO TS G
FJ22 LONDON T 8 24 1130

LUCKY ESTRAGON
PSOPHIDIAN LONDON

DEFINITELY ARRIVING THURSDAY

GODOT

299992 PO TS G
299858 PO WD G

Dear Doctor Holliday,

I really must insist that you attend to my husband. I have now called five times at your shack to ask you to come out and look at him. Twice I have found you unconscious in a pool of whiskey and on the other three occasions I was told you were at the saloon with Mr. Earp.

People in this town are beginning to ask if you have abandoned your medical practice altogether. If not, you are shamefully neglecting it. I hear tell that when Jim Dawson was shot in a brawl you said on the death certificate that the cause of death was "lead poisoning".

If you cannot come to see my husband I will come in and pick up a prescription for his stomach pain. Please meet me tomorrow morning. As you know, we live a little way out, but I will drive in and I suggest you meet me at ten o'clock at the OK Corral.

Don't forget—ten o'clock prompt, OK Corral. And be sober.

Yours, etc.,

(Mrs) Jessica Smith

High Street,
Nottingham
Jan. 18, 1235

Dear Robin,

No, no, you can't possibly dress the Merrie Men in orange jackets and mauve leggings with yellow cross-gartering, and I absolutely forbid you to make them wear those little red hats. To start with, apart from the hideous colours, they'll stand out like beacons in the forest and will all get picked off by the soldiers. Also, no self-respecting stag would stay within bowshot of someone creeping up on it dressed in a red hat and mauve leggings. I suspect this ridiculous idea has been put up by Will Scarlett.

Incidentally, I don't think it's a good idea, either, to put your monogram on your arrows. Then the sheriff will know who shot him.

What you want is a sensible outfit in Lincoln Green, with a nice curly hat with a feather in it and brown shoes. We might put brown edging round the jackets and scallop the bottoms. I will make one for Sunday and bring it to the Forest and you can try it on someone, preferably not Little John or Will Scarlett. As usual, by the third oak from the left at the cross-roads.

With love,

Marion

The Garrick Club,
London WC1
July 21st, 1865

John Wilkes Booth Esq.,
State Penitentiary,
Washington, U.S.A.

Dear Booth,

What has gotten into you to shoot that harmless old man and before the interval, too? And what on earth made you pick one of my plays to do it in? You have ruined what promised to be one of my best pieces. How can anyone perform *Our American Cousin* in future, or to be more accurate how are they ever going to get past Act One, Scene Two? At a recent performance in London, as the fatal moment when President Lincoln was shot approached, the entire audience turned round and were looking up at the box on the prompt side, which was where the President was sitting when you shot him with callousness one would have expected from a literary agent or publisher, not from a member of the theatrical profession. To make matters worse, a bottle of beer exploded at that moment and 35 people fainted. Naturally, the performance was ruined.

What is happening now is that audiences are demanding we do not put on the play without a representation of the assassination, complete with an actor leaping on to the stage in imitation of your ridiculous posturing after the firing of the shot. As someone said to me the other night, "The killing of the President was the best thing in your play, Mr. Taylor."

Permit me to tell you Booth, that you have seriously let down the profession, not to mention wrecking my career as a playwright. People are already referring to me not as the author of *The Ticket-of-Leave Man* but as the man who wrote the play they shot Lincoln in. I trust you realise the harm you have done.

Yours faithfully,

Tom Taylor

Dear Brother,

You are an uncle at last and your nephew is a lovely little boy but we had an extraordinary time of it. To start with, because everywhere was full up when we got here we had to stay in the stable of an inn, and the baby was born there. It wasn't too uncomfortable, and we put the baby in a manger for a cradle, which was very convenient. Fortunately, all went smoothly and Mary and I were just trying to get some sleep after an extremely tiring day when suddenly the door burst open and three shepherds marched in. They were a bit incoherent as to exactly why they had come—something about while watching their flocks by night a great light came down and told them to go to the stable. Well, we were as polite as possible under the circumstances and let them see the baby—which immediately woke up, of course—and then dropped a few hints that we were tired, and we all bade a polite farewell. By now we were absolutely exhausted and we'd just settled down to sleep again when there was a tremendous knocking on the stable door. I got up in rather a bad temper and when I opened it there were three weird old men standing outside. I've never seen such peculiar characters in all my life. As soon as I let them in they all started pointing at the baby and babbling at each other. And they then all fell on their knees in front of the manger, after which they started muttering something about Herod. Then they got up and believe it or not, they went outside to their camels and carried in three barrels of frankincense and two casks of myrrh, altogether weighing about half a ton I suppose, which they asked me to give to the baby.

I ask you—what does an ordinary man-in-the-street do with three barrels of frankincense and two casks of myrrh? Actually, I'm not quite sure what they're used for anyway. I've an idea they use myrrh for embalming people but we haven't got anyone around here who needs embalming at present. As regards the frankincense, for the present I'm treating it as a deodorant and putting a little under my arms each morning but at that rate it's going to take fifty years to use this lot. Mary says she will try to use some of the myrrh in cooking when she is stronger.

I really do think it was a bit inconsiderate of the old geezers. People should think before they do these things. Still, in fairness to them, they did leave a little gold as well, not much, but just enough to pay for our lodging here and it was nice of them to think of the baby.

By the time they had gone we were quite worn out but we still couldn't get any peace. For the rest of the night, our sleep, what there was of it, was constantly interrupted by a chorus of strange music from somewhere up above and the beating of wings as if bloody great birds were hovering around the stable. I told the landlord about it next morning and said it was like sleeping next door to an aviary. Believe me, I've had enough of Bethlehem. I think I shall take Mary and the baby to Egypt for a little peace and quiet.

Still, the baby is absolutely gorgeous, a really sweet child. The only thing that worries us is that sometimes he appears to have a ring of bright light around his head, but Mary says he will grow out of it.

Meanwhile, do you know anyone who wants three barrels of frankincense and two casks of myrrh? I really don't feel like dragging them about with us but they must be of some use to someone somewhere.

Yours affectionately,

Joseph

Dear Concordia,

I would like to ask a favour of you. As you know, the gallant Pheidippides ran more than 26 miles from the battlefield at Marathon recently to bring the great news that the Persian army had been completely defeated there. Having delivered his message in the market place to the assembled elders, his great spirit failed and he died upon the spot.

Naturally he will be greatly honoured. A statue in his memory will be erected before the temple of Apollo and his widow will receive as much land as ten oxen can plough in a week. But it is about his widow I wish to write. As you are a good friend of hers, I seek your help.

The fact is, poor Pheidippides died in vain. We already knew the Persians had been defeated as another messenger had come on a horse and told us. Actually, it wouldn't have been difficult to get there ahead of Pheidippides as he got lost on the way and took nearly twelve hours anyway. Some of the common people made rough jests at him as he tottered across the square, calling out, "What delayed you, chum?" and "Where's your horse, mate?" Mercifully the poor fellow was too exhausted to heed these and simply gasped out his message before sinking to the ground. Even then, he didn't deliver it all. He was so far gone, all he could do was to pant, "News my lords. The Persians have been defeated at aaaaaarrrrrgggghhhhhh!" With which he gave a loud cry, clutched his chest, and sank down. Fortunately, they knew the result of the battle already, so it didn't matter.

I am very anxious that his widow should not know he died uselessly so I am asking you to shield her from the gossip which may reach her ears. You could say the story about the other messenger getting there first was spread by jealous people. Do this and the gods will bless you.

Meanwhile, we are instituting an annual race in memory of Pheidippides to keep his heroic example before the people. The course will be just over 26 miles long, the same distance that he covered from Marathon (we won't count the bit where he got lost) and the race will be known as The Pheidippides. I hope this will perpetuate his memory and that thousands of years hence men will still be running a race of 26 miles and calling it A Pheidippides.

Yours,

Cleon

Your Majesty,

Your faithful Raleigh sends loyal greetings on his
return from the expedition to the Americas and begs
you to accept these small gifts as tokens of affection
for England's Virgin Queen Elizabeth, after whom
has been named a portion of the newly-discovered
territory overseas, viz. the land of Virginia.

The first package contains some curious stones
and so forth found upon the shores of that distant
land. The second contains ornaments and weapons
used by the rude inhabitants, wild savages who live
in tall, conical tents but who were friendly to us and
whom I made swear allegiance to Your Majesty.

The third package contains my greatest discovery.
It is a root, which grows in great profusion in the
Americas, and needs little cultivation. It is called
there The Potato and is used by the American
savages in a remarkable manner. First of all, the
Potato is skinned with a sharp knife, so only the
white flesh is visible and the rough outside removed.
It is then cut into thin strips and dried and stuffed
into containers on the end of long clay pipes, hollow
so air may be drawn through. The Potato is then lit
with a live coal and the smoke drawn through the
tube into the lungs and mouth of the smoker, as he is
called, which gives a pleasant and beneficial feeling.
Many of the savages also believe that this Potato will
cure diseases, and certainly they smoke it all day long
with no ill-effects. It is also used as a ceremonial way
of celebrating a peace treaty, both parties smoking a
pipe together.

The fourth cask contains another substance
peculiar to the Americas, viz. a brown leaf called
The Tobacco, which grows on small bushes

plentifully. The manner of preparing this is to pick the leaves, dry them, compress them into a block and then boil them for half an hour with large quantities of salt. The Tobacco is then taken out of the pot and drained and may be served with roast meats and other viands. It is improved if parsley is sprinkled on it. Sometimes the Tobacco is pulped with a fork after boiling, with the addition of a little milk. Another way of preparing Tobacco is to cut the compressed leaves into small oblong pieces and fry them in grease or oil. These are particularly pleasant served with fish or with eggs and the cured flesh of wild hogs.

That Your Majesty may sample the delights of these new foods, hitherto unknown in Christendom, I shall prepare tomorrow evening a feast in which The Tobacco shall be served in several ways, both boiled, pulped with milk and fried, together with various meats and salads and so forth. Then, at the conclusion of the banquet Your Majesty shall be presented with a pipe and together we shall sample the heavenly pleasures of inhaling The Potato Smoke.

> Floreat Regina!
> Your Majesty's devoted slave,
>
> Raleigh

Greenwich
March 10, 1585

My dear Cecil,
    Pray have Sir Walter Raleigh conveyed to the
Tower and send for my physician.

        Elizabeth R.

26

Dear Colonel Gorski,

In sending you yesterday a list of people to be executed for crimes against the state I accidentally included the name of my mother, to whom I was writing a birthday card at the time. I would be grateful if you could delete her name from the list.

If the execution has already been carried out, kindly send stock postcard of condolences No. 4 (close relatives) and then add your own name to the list.

Yours sincerely,

J. V. Stalin (comrade)

299858 PO WD G
299992 PO TS G
DA40 1820 CORK DN S/A S/RISK 12/11

LUCKY ESTRAGON
PSOPHIDIAN
LONDON

SLIGHT DELAY STOP WILL CONTACT SOONEST
GODOT

COL PSOPHIDIAN GODOT
299992 PO TS G
299858 PO WD G

Stonehenge
B.C. 1567

Mr Lord Archdruid,

    I have to tell you that the hostel project has fallen through. The architect planned accommodation for 500 visitors to the Summer Solstice celebrations here. It was an interesting circular design, but the constructors had only got as far as building doorposts when money ran out. So we have a ring of stone doorposts. I do not know what we can do with them.

    I await further instructions.

            Yours faithfully,

            Uffa the Wise
            Wiltshire Lodge

Der Konzerthaus,
Vienna
Jan. 18, 1816

Dear Mr. Schubert,
    I wish to protest in the strongest possible manner about your latest composition, which has just been delivered to me. The symphony is all right so far as it goes, but it appears to be incomplete. You have not bothered to finish it.

    Believe me, Mr. Schubert, nobody is ever going to listen to an incomplete piece of music, let alone pay good money to do so. I cannot understand what has come over you. Is this some form of blackmail for increased fees? You have not complained of being underpaid before. We are at a loss.

    I am returning the work and I regret that I shall have to withhold all payment for it until you have added the final part of the last movement. When that is done I would be glad if you could give the work a title, which is at present lacking.

    If I may offer a word of personal advice, Mr. Schubert, you must pull yourself together and do better than this. If you cannot be bothered to complete pieces nobody is going to trouble with your music.

            Yours sincerely,

            A. Haupmann
            Direktor

Dear Mrs. Washington,

I do not wish to appear un-neighbourly, but good grief what on earth possessed you to give your son George an axe for Christmas? As you know, we have a little spinney at the bottom of our garden. I think it would be more correct to say we used to have a little spinney at the bottom of our garden. This morning, when I went for a walk before breakfast, I found the whole wood laid flat. Every tree but one had been chopped down. It was as if the trees had been attacked by someone with superhuman strength.

As I say, one tree was left and that was at the instant of being felled by your son, who was wielding his axe in a frenzy. Paying no attention to my protests he completed his work and I only escaped by a fraction of an inch as it crashed to the ground.

I will tell you something else, Mrs. Washington. That son of yours is a liar. When I spoke to him I said, "George Washington, landsakes, what has come over you to do this terrible thing?" and he looked kind of shifty and then he said, "My maw told me to do it." I told him I'm sure his maw never told him to do any such thing and he blushed and said no, she didn't tell him, he did it himself because the trees were diseased. I guess this annoyed me so I shook him and said, "George Washington you cannot tell the truth. You took your axe and chopped down my cherry trees," and at this his eyes began staring and foam came out of his mouth and he said, "The axe is laid to the root of the trees. The day has come!" And I said, "It sure has, young Washington, you have just destroyed two hundred dollars' worth of woodland. I am going to speak to your maw about this."

But that isn't all. At that moment his eyes lighted on the privy near my fence and with a ghastly cry he ran towards the building and demolished it with one sweep of his axe. It is a mercy no one was inside at the time. I then felt it wiser to retire inside and I am sending our Abigail with this note.

We have enough trouble with the British soldiers and Excisemen around here without your son adding to it. Why doesn't he put his energies to something useful, like young Paul Revere down the road, who has taught himself to ride at the age of 3? Believe me, that boy of yours will come to no good.

Yours

Ebenezer Judd

Downing Street,
London,
England.
April 29, 1855

Dear Ferdinand de Lesseps,

As you know, H.M. Government have just purchased a large number of shares in the Suez Canal Company. However, I am rather worried about something. Your proposed canal is nearly 100 miles long. Have you allowed for the curvature of the earth over that distance? As I see it, each end of the canal will be about 100 feet below the level of the centre portion, due to the earth's curvature. This would mean that the water would drain away at each end, leaving a large hump of dry land in the middle.

I hope you will forgive this presumption, but £10,000,000 is a lot of money to invest.

Yours faithfully,

Benj. Disraeli
Prime Minister

Dear Francis,

Just a line to ask if you have any more like that
one about the Danish Prince? They are crying out
for more stuff up here in London but I have used up
that Italian joke book you sent me and in any case
the plots were nearly all the same, mostly about
twins getting mixed up and so forth. There's a limit
to what you can do with twins. But when I told
Burbage about the Danish lad he thought it was the
finest thing since pickled herrings. I promise you
will get full credit and a share of the proceeds, as
sure as my name's Will Shakspeer. The name Bacon
will appear immediately underneath mine. I swear it.
May I go bald if I do not fulfil this promise.

Love's Labours Won did terrible business and I
shall have to rewrite it with a different plot. Have
you any ideas as to how I might change the end? I'm
afraid *Nine Gentlemen of Verona* did no better, in fact
it only lasted one night. One of the groundlings
actually peed on the stage to show his disapproval.
This will be another rewrite job, I'm afraid. I'm
under pressure from Burbage to reduce the number
of men involved since we only have eight altogether
and one found himself playing fourteen parts. *A
Midsummer Night's Dream* wasn't too bad except
that the boy who played Hermia kept scratching his
arse and Will Kemp was dreadful as Bottom,
overdoing it, gagging and writing-in his own lines.
He actually invented a line, "There is not a more
fearful wild-fowl than your lion living." What stupid
piffle! As if I would write a line like that (or you for
that matter).

Now one or two queries about your draft of the

35

Danish play. This hero of yours called Omlet (is that right by the way? Your writing is awful) has far too many long speeches, mostly talking to himself. And I can't think of an ending, any more than you can. At present I've got Omlet leading an army to attack the king's castle at Elsinore. They go through a wood and hew down branches to hide themselves. Meanwhile, in the castle, the Queen has gone mad and dies, while Claudius buckles on his armour in the belief he cannot be slain by any man born of woman.

I somehow feel this isn't quite right. Have you got any of your brilliant suggestions? I think we should have a happy ending, with the Ghost suddenly appearing and saying, "Hullo everybody, I'm not really the old king's ghost, I'm alive, the poison missed my ear and went down my neck. But I thought I'd pretend to be dead to see what happened." And then he would forgive his wife, banish Claudius and hand over the throne to young Omlet. How do you feel about that?

If you could solve this one we have a winner, and the combination of Bacon and Shakspere will become famous. I know up to now you've seen no reward for your efforts, but honestly I promise that this time you'll get full credit. The five shillings you wrote about is in the post.

Rely on me.

Your old friend,
Will

Obergruppenführers Büro
Berlin

27th February
1933

Heidi—
I left a cigarette burning
on Martin Bormann's desk
in the Reichstag. If
there's any damage, I'll
pay.
Hermann

37

Chère Sophie,

I just had to write to you as I have a wonderful design to help the poor people of Paris. As you know, there has been a lot of trouble recently and on Tuesday there was the most terrible commotion outside the Palace gates. So I came downstairs, although it was only eleven o'clock, and so did Louis and there outside the gates were absolutely hordes of people. There must have been ten thousand of them, chèrie, and they were shouting and banging the gates and some of them were firing fusils and muskets. So Louis asks the chamberlain what is the matter and the chamberlain replies, "They say they have no bread, sire," and Louis orders the guards to disperse them and goes upstairs to continue cataloguing his clocks.

But I, I am so soft-hearted that I think to myself how terrible it is that the poor people of Paris should have no bread to eat, and then this wonderful idea, he come to me. If there is no bread, why should they not eat cake? And so, chèrie, I thought I would write to my favourite patisserie, which is yours chèrie, and beg you to do something about it, viz. you shall load a cart with macaroons or cream horns and you shall take it into the poorest districts and you shall sell them to the populace and they will be happy and will not come to the Palace gates to worry poor Louis and me. Alas, poor Louis, he have so many troubles. Yesterday the spring broke on his favourite clock. Today he is ill in bed with his old trouble, gold poisoning. The doctor says he must use china cups in future. Nobody realises the cross he has to bear.

Your eternal friend,

Marie Antoinette

38

Aboard H.M.S. Victory
October 20, 1805

From the Rt. Hon. Lord Viscount Nelson,
Commander in Chief

Dear Hardy,

I have been in conversation with the Surgeon concerning the unfortunate effect of a restricted diet upon the health of the seamen. This long blockade of the Spanish coast has resulted in the exhaustion of almost all fresh supplies and the people are living upon a regimen of salt pork and split peas. Mercifully, we have few cases of scurvy but an even more terrible scourge is now inflicting itself upon the Fleet, a veritable blockade of the inward parts. It seems impervious to the strongest purgatives—even rhubarb pills have no effect—and must eventually affect the health of the crews and working of the fleet unless checked.

I feel it is partly caused by lack of *regularity* (as you know, these things are the result of habit more than anything else). If the people could be brought to a habit of regularity in this then I believe the trouble would disappear. I therefore intend to signal the whole Fleet tomorrow morning with the intention of instilling such a habit and I would be grateful if you would prepare a signal to be hoisted at four bells in the morning watch. I would suggest ALL CREWS TO THE HEADS THIS DAY or perhaps something with a more patriotic appeal, viz. ENGLAND EXPECTS THAT EVERY MAN THIS DAY WILL DO HIS DUTY.

All ships to acknowledge and execute forthwith.

If all indeed do their duty in this respect our troubles will be over and health and happiness restored to our gallant seamen.

Pray do not trouble yourself about the enemy. I do not expect to meet the French and Spanish for some time yet, if at all. I do not think we shall bring them to action this year.

Nelson

My Lord Mayor,

As Clerk to the Parish of Billingsgate it is my
melancholy duty to explain to you the circumstances
surrounding the recent Great Fire which destroyed
the City of London, since the aforesaid conflagration
began in this parish.

On the evening of September 2, in the Year of Our
Lord 1666, I was dining at the house of some friends
in Mark Lane when a woman came running to the
door crying that a cow had kicked over a lantern in
her stable at the baker's house in Pudding Lane and
that no one could put it out and she was afeard the
stable and house and all would catch alight.

On the instant I rose from my plate of anchovies
and knocked up the Watch, which consisted of
Crippled Jack, Wheezing William, Blind Jacob and
Dumb Daniel, telling Wheezing William to get
assistance to fetch the parish fire engine from the
house of Widow Jackson to pump water on to the
flames from the river. On reaching the baker's house
we percvd. it to be already well alight so I sent Blind
Jacob to tell Wheezing William to hasten, the while
myself and Dumb Daniel poured water on the flames
with buckets.

Alas, the buckets being full of holes and the river
some yards away, they were empty by the time we
had brought them to the house and our only hope lay
in the speedy arrival of the engine. But so much for
mortal hopes, My Lord. That Power Above, who
giveth and taketh away, had ordained otherwise. For
although Blind Jacob knows his way about the City
like a sighted man, he must first be pointed in the
right direction, and what with the confusion of the

fire and the cries and alarms, he was pointed the wrong way and urged to make all haste, which he did, and duly walked straight into the river. Seeing this, Dumb Daniel ran after him to pull him out, so that I alone was fighting the flames.

Meanwhile Wheezing William had failed to get any help with the parish engine and no answer to his entreaties except insults, this being because he owes money to everyone in the parish. So he was compelled to pull the engine to the scene of the fire by himself, to the jeers of the populace. Thus it took him a half-hour to reach the conflagration. When he did so, he was exhausted and stopped to rest for a moment, leaving the engine while he went to relieve himself. But sad to relate, My Lord, Pudding Lane, as you know, is on a slope and when he turned to resume his task the engine was rolling down towards the river, into which it plunged, knocking down Dumb Daniel just as he was rescuing Blind Jacob, and hurling both of them back into the river Thames, where they were joined by Wheezing William, who was pursuing the engine.

What feeling of trepidation lodged in my bosom could now be imagined. For by now the whole street was in flames, and the fire engine and three of its attendants all in the river. This left only Crippled Jack to help, who was little enough use, and even that small help was taken, for shortly after the engine plunged into the Thames I percvd. that Crippled Jack's wooden leg had caught fire and he was hopping around like a mad thing trying to beat out the flames. But alas, he could not reach the end of his leg and with a wild shriek he hobbled down the hill and jumped into the river like a flaming dart, landing upon Dumb Daniel, Wheezing William and Blind Jacob, who were all trying to clamber out for the second time, and hurling them back into the stream.

42

Thus Wheezing William, Dumb Daniel, Blind Jacob and Crippled Jack, together with the parish fire engine, were now all in the Thames, and still the flames rose higher and higher.

I then percvd. that nearby was a warehouse full of barrels which I took to contain beer and I conceived the notion that we might put out the flames by pouring the contents of the barrels on to the blaze, which now threatened the next street. Aided by one or two men who had not lent Wheezing William any money, I carried a barrel back to Pudding Lane. But once more that Great Arbiter Above decided to mock our plans. For when the barrel had been carried to the fire, and the end smashed in and it was hurled on to the blaze, it transpired it was full of brandy, which immediately caught fire and flowed in a flaming torrent through the street, setting fire to five more houses, and driving Wheezing William, Dumb Daniel, Crippled Jack and Blind Jacob back into the river from which they were emerging.

My Lord, I can write no more. Suffice to say the fire raged for three days as you well know, and nothing at all survived its fury except the parish fire engine, which was preserved from the flames through running into the river Thames. Thus out of evil cometh good, and with a little grease it will be as good as new. But otherwise all tidings are bad. Blind Jacob has lost his coat, Crippled Jack his wooden leg, St. Paul's Cathedral is burned down, ten thousand people are without homes and I am feeling unwell myself.

Your humble servant,

Jeremiah Bidewell,
Clerk to the Parish

ADDENDUM: My Lord, we are but poor men

and suffered deeply in the Fire. I lost my anchovy supper and a pair of good shoes, together with my hat. I have told of Blind Jacob and Crippled Jack. Also, Dumb Daniel lost his spectacles and Wheezing William lost his purse, although all the money in it had been borrowed. If Your Lordship should feel moved in his wisdom to forward the sum of £10 he would make five poor men grateful to him for life.

ZCZC CLF1560 LBE723 ELB1788 OAC907 TL424
GBXX HL AASU 015
ST JAMES NSW 15 11 1500
   LT
   LUCKY ESTRAGON PSOPHIDIAN
   LONDONW1

SORRY ABOUT THURSDAY STOP WILL COME

FRIDAY WITHOUT FAIL

        GODOT

   TX UR 299858 AB 299858 G
   MO SA 0215-1900
   TX UR 298111 AB 298111 G SU 001-1700

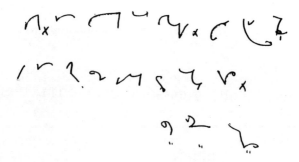

Isaac Pitman

(Translation:

Help. I am locked in the lavatory. Will the finder of this note which I am dropping from the window please inform the police.

Sir Isaac Pitman)

Windsor
Feb. 8, 1859

Dear Albert,

I wish you would speak to that *odious* Mr.
Disraeli. He has been *forward* again.

Yesterday he told me a story of *such bad taste* that
I blush to repeat it, but I fear I must do so, in order
that you can form your own opinion of his *impropriety*.

During his audience, conversation happened to
turn upon certain events in South America and Mr.
Disraeli said talking of South America reminded him
of a rather amusing story which would make me
burst my stays. Before I could stop him he launched
forth, and said the story concerned a peasant girl in
Brazil, who was working on a coffee plantation.
Alongside her was working a young man and one day
the young man seized the girl in his arms and *kissed
her* (!!!).

At this point I *begged* Mr. Disraeli to desist in the
name of all modesty but he *insisted* on finishing,
saying he had not yet got to the best bit and when he
did *I would be in stitches*.

As the girl and the man were embracing, the
proprietor of the plantation rode up on his horse and
demanded of the young man, "What grounds have
you for kissing that girl?"

The young man replied, "Coffee grounds".

At the termination of this narrative Mr. Disraeli
collapsed on the floor *crying with mirth* and had to be
helped from the room, calling out "Coffee grounds!"
and *laughing immoderately*.

I told him, "We are not amused, Mr. Disraeli" but
I think it would be as well if you were to have a word
with him also. His behaviour is becoming as *offensive*
as that Mr. Gladstone, who *never* listens to what
I say.

Victoria R. I.

Dear Leonardo,

I am afraid I shall have to rearrange the sitting I was due to have tomorrow morning. I have to go to the surgeon to have my teeth examined, so I will postpone the sitting until the evening, when I will have completed my appointment with him. He says he may have to take out one of my front teeth but it should not make much difference to my expression.

Yours sincerely,

Lisa

103, Appian Way,
Rome
March 10

Dear Julius,

I wonder if you would like to come for a picnic
with us on March 15th? We are planning to drive to
Ostia in my new chariot, the one with four horses.
There will just be me and Lavinia, plus the servants
of course, and we thought it would be lovely if you
and Calpurnia came along. Bring the palace guard if
you like.

If it will tempt you, for lunch we are having lion.
It was thrown to the gladiators the other day.
Lavinia has marinated it and we are going to have it
cold with pickles. Lavinia says you can have the tail.
You always liked that, didn't you?

Do come, old chap. It's such a long time since we
got away from it all.

Your old friend,

Flavius Tribunus

Caesar's Palace,
Rome
March 11th

Dear Flavius,

Many thanks for the kind invitation. I would
have loved to come but I'm afraid I simply have to
go to the Senate on March 15. They have a lot of
urgent business to discuss, such as all the people
throwing up their sweaty nightcaps and leaving them
in the streets where they get wrapped round the

49

chariot wheels. Also, there are a large number of petitions to be delivered, I believe. And between you and me old chap, there's just a possibility of them offering me that crown but mum's the word. Anyway, Cassius and Brutus in particular are very anxious that I should be there, so I really ought to go.

However, I would love to come on another day. How about March 16th? I shall be doing absolutely nothing that day except lying around.

Kind regards,

Julius

Dear Sophos,

I really must ask that you come and attend to our plumbing as quickly as possible. The new hot water system you fitted is completely out of control. Yesterday my son went to take his daily bath as usual and I thought nothing more of it until I was startled by a terrible shout of pain from upstairs. The poor boy had jumped into the bath without testing the temperature of the water (I'm afraid he is rather preoccupied and absent-minded, like most scholars) and was now running round the house shrieking "Oh my God, eureka . . . eureka!" in his agony and begging someone to throw cold water over him. He really is quite badly scalded and is unable to conduct the experiments he was working on concerning the displacement of bodies immersed in water.

Please come and fix the holocaust so this doesn't happen again. I always said that new design from Rome was no good.

Yours sincerely,

Z. Archimedes (Mrs.)

Dear Mr. Caxton,

What are you doing to my monastery? We were
founded some four hundred years ago for the express
purpose of copying out the Bible. There are about
100 monks here, and we take great pride in our work,
with the result that in 400 years we have produced
eleven Bibles, and have every hope of completing
another twenty before the next Millennium. We take
special pride in the high quality of our artistic work.
Indeed, Bro. Francis has just spent six months on
the first letter of the third chapter of The Book of
Job (which is an A by the way). Bro. Joseph spent his
whole life on one chapter of Leviticus and died
before it could be completed.

Now your new invention will make all our work
useless. Who will want to wait for one of our Bibles
when he can order a copy from your goodself and
have the same delivered from stock or else printed in
a few weeks? I am afraid all the heart has gone out of
the monks. Bro. Francis doesn't understand printing
and thinks books are produced by teams of ten
thousand men with little pens, and says we could do
the same if we recruited ten thousand more monks,
but he is a little simple, poor old soul.

There is no other task we are fit for but copying.
There is little land attached to the Abbey and we
have no skill in cultivation. Bro. John tried to make
wine from our wild gooseberries to raise money, but
it poisoned everybody. Bro. Francis painted a
portrait of the King and sent it to him, but he only
threatened to dissolve the Order. Unless we can copy
out Bibles there is no reason for us to exist at all, a
fact that has already been noted by several barons
who would like our property.

Mr. Caxton, examine your conscience before you proceed further.

Yours in God,

Dominic, D.O.M.

021531

ZCZC TXE7882 EOF521 AWD0857 1714

GBXX CO AUWX 023

WIEN/TEL 23 2 1605

PERSONAL TO HER MAJESTY'S PRINCIPAL
SECRETARY OF STATE FOR FOREIGN AFFAIRS
FOREIGN OFFICE KING CHARLES STREET
LONDON/SW1

REGRET UNABLE VISIT SARAJEVO

ARCHDUKE FERDINAND

COL LONDON/SW1

21, Rue Montmartre,
Paris
Dec. 3, 1889

The Chairman,
Committee for the Construction of the Eiffel Tower,
Paris

Sir,
　　Recently I have been away from Paris and unable
to see the construction of the tower which I designed
and which bears my name. I have to tell you that
when I visited the site yesterday my feelings were
those of indescribable horror! A formidable mistake
has been made by the engineer in charge. He is
building the tower upside down!
　　My design called for a tower of iron girders with a
small base supporting a long slender column which
widened out at the top like a lovely flower. It would
have been a structure unique in the history of the
world's architecture. The widest part would have
been at the top, where there would have been ample
space for an immense area to promenade or even to
play games. Indeed, it was my dream that perhaps
one day cycling, athletics and other sports would be
held at the top of the Eiffel Tower. In time of war
the top platform might have been used as a parade
ground for troops stationed there to shoot down
enemy balloons.
　　Imagine my feelings of desolation when on
visiting the site I discovered the imbecile in charge
had got the plan the wrong way up and had been
working on the false notion that the tower would
have a broad base and gradually taper as it got
towards the top, culminating in a narrow pinnacle.
　　I pointed out the error in the strongest terms.
"Name of a dog," I said, "Why do you not complete

your travesty properly, and put a Metro station at the top? Or perhaps we could put the lightning conductors at the base?" Alas, like all idiots, he is impervious to argument and said they had gone too far now to alter it and personally he believed it was better like this in any case, as it would overbalance the other way.

I must warn you, sir, that in fact there is a serious safety risk in the present structure. My original design had the lines of force from the top storey falling outside the base and thus creating stability. As the tower is now being constructed, these lines will fall inside the base and the structure will be most unsafe in high winds, being liable to collapse inwards upon itself. However, as no one will bother to visit a tower that has been built upside down this is hardly likely to matter.

My distinguished sentiments,

Gustave Eiffel

Cherry Farm,
Washington,
Virginia
August 5, 1752

Dear Benjamin Franklin,

I am returning the remains of your kite, which was found in my oak tree after your unfortunate accident last Saturday. If I may say so, I do not think it is a very safe thing to do to fly a kite in a thunderstorm. However, I hope you have recovered from the effects of the explosion by now and that your hair will grow again. I also enclose some ointment Mrs. Franklin may find soothing for her burns. If you need any timber for rebuilding, you have only to ask.

Yours sincerely,

Abe Wetherhead

P.S.   There is no need to pay for the hogs. We were going to kill them anyway, although not in such a spectacular fashion.

The Bourse,
Paris
March 5, 1883

Dear Mr. Gauguin,

What are you thinking of? As your partner I beg you to give up this foolishness and return to the office. You were always so happy here and everyone respected your artistic nature. Nobody complained when you painted the ceiling of the office with nude women.

You have a natural talent for business which God gave you and you have no right to neglect it. I never knew anyone who could forecast the whim of the stock market better or who was sharper and shrewder on a deal. You also wrote such a neat hand and could add up rapidly. If Nature gives you these great gifts, who are you to throw them away?

But perhaps, Paul, you are not so foolish after all. Maybe you felt you were not getting a big enough percentage, eh? And this is your way of reminding me? How I admire your cunning! Well, you have won your point, you rogue. Your commission on turnover will in future be increased by a further 10 per cent. I do not think the Paul Gauguin that I knew and respected will be able to resist a magic ten per cent.

I confidently look forward to seeing you in the office on Monday. Bring along one of your little pictures with you. My wife needs one for the spare bedroom.

Yours sincerely,

Alfonse Beaujolais

Dear Ralph,

I do not know if you will receive this since I am
entrusting it to a gentleman with a bone through his
nose who promises to carry it to the Great Canoe
With Fire Inside and it may eventually get home to
you in the good old U.S.A. But I am writing it so
that you, as my oldest friend, will know what has
happened to me now I am reported dead, as I must
surely be.

As you know, we sailed from New York last
November, bound for Genoa with a cargo of alcohol
in barrels. Just after we had passed the Azores, I was
lying in my bunk off-watch when I was awoken by a
terrible hollering and screeching. So I got up and
found the mate dragging a beautiful black girl from
the hold, where she had stowed away. My, she was
so pretty I fell in love with her at first sight and I
guess everyone in the crew did, but that didn't stop
the mate dragging her to the stern and locking her up
while he told the captain. And that was the last I saw
of her for some days until I happened to have the
midnight watch and what should I see but the black
girl—whose name was Semolina—and the captain
embracing behind the chart-house. Then the mate
came round the corner of the chart-house, took one
look at the scene and sprang at the captain with a cry
of, "Leave her alone, she's mine I tell you!" For a
moment they struggled in silence and then the mate,
who was a giant of a man, lifted up the captain and
threw him overboard. I guess his neck was broken
for he never surfaced and then the mate turns and
sees me standing frozen with horror by the wheel.
He strode across and put his face close to mine and
snarled, "You saw nothing. Mind that, you saw

59

nothing." With that he seizes the terrified girl and goes below.

Next day the mate gives out the captain had disappeared in the night and bold as brass installs the black girl in his own cabin. And I said nothing because I was afraid of the mate, but the crew knew the truth all right and the bosun, a huge Scotsman named Macneil, said it was a shame a pretty girl like that should be forced to live with such a murdering brute as the mate. I think he was sweet on the girl himself. At any rate, two mornings later I came on deck to find the mate face downwards with Macneil's knife between his shoulder blades and Macneil kissing the girl passionately. When he saw me his hand flew to his knife, but it was buried in the mate's back, so he contented himself with snarling, "You saw nothing. Remember that, you saw nothing," and by now I was getting used to that and I said OK, I saw nothing.

Macneil threw the mate overboard and gave out he went mad and jumped over the side, which left Macneil in charge of the ship, and he moved into the captain's cabin with the girl. Only this girl had turned more than a few heads, and three nights later I was at the wheel when Paddy O'Connor, a huge Irishman in the crew, tip-toed past me with a marlin spike in his hand, and then there was a cry from the cabin below, and he returned dragging the girl by the waist.

By now we were having difficulty in navigating, since the only three men who understood it were dead and the ship was sailing round in circles. Paddy O'Connor appointed himself captain and moved in with the girl for two days, when I found him on deck with his head caved in and there behind the mizzen mast was Slim Jackson, a smart Yankee from Boston, kissing the girl like mad, and Slim sees me and starts to speak, but I get in quick and say, "I saw nothing, Slim, I saw nothing." He nods, but even as he nodded a shot rang out and he staggered back dead, and Ebenezer Jones, the cook, stands there with a smoking pistol and seizes the girl with a shout of triumph and drags her below. But his triumph don't last long since ten minutes later there is another shot and Ed Ford comes up the companionway dragging Ebenezer after him and throws him into the sea and then goes below with a shout of "Darling, I'm a-coming for you."

By the time another three days had passed there were only two crew left—me and Fats Maggio. The last to go were Jim Ridgeway and Big Bill Walters, who strangled each other and both fell dead on deck.

That left me, Fats and the girl. I grabbed an axe and shinned up the mizzen mast for safety and then I heard a hollering from the mainmast where Fats had shinned so *I* couldn't get at *him*. We had a talk by shouting across the rigging and Fats said he wasn't interested in the girl, leastways, not if it meant getting killed, and I said the same so we came down to decide what to do.

I wanted to signal another ship but Fats and the girl said no, we shall be hanged for mutiny. I guess it *is* a little difficult for a jury to believe that the ship's officers all murdered each other, and then the crew did likewise, especially when the story's told by two common seamen and a nigger. So we held a farewell party by stoving in some of the casks of alcohol and cooked a farewell meal and got into the longboat, leaving most of the food still warm on the galley stove. We set a course for Africa, the ship abandoned with all sail set and nothing to show what had happened to the crew.

For three months we've lived in a native village near the coast, cut off from civilisation but quite

61

happy. I live with Semolina in one hut and Fats has shacked up with a native girl in another. For all purposes we are dead to the world, and we prefer it that way. But I'm sending this letter to you, old friend, so one person will know the real truth.

Oh, by the way, I never told you the name of the ship. She was *The Marie Celeste*. I don't suppose you've ever heard of her.

Your friend,

Jack Slade

Instituto Ibérico de Arte,
Avenida Cristobal Colón,
Barcelona,
July 9, 1897

Dear Mr. Picasso,

    I am very worried about your son's attitude to biology and I am writing to ask if you could acquaint him with some of the more elementary facts of life. This term we began to study human anatomy with the final year students and we use this biological knowledge as an introduction to the mysteries of procreation, since most of the boys in that class will be leaving school shortly.

    Your son has been studious and hard-working but when it came to the examinations it appeared he did not have the remotest idea of how the human frame works, or even what it looks like. Asked to draw a diagram of the blood flow in a human being, he placed one arm on top of the figure's head, and had the feet facing backwards. In another diagram he represented a person as having a triangular face. His worst effort, however, was when he had to draw the female organs of reproduction. These were placed behind the left ear. They were square and had a large eye peering out of them. Some of his diagrams show the female breasts detached and floating in the air.

    Plainly, there are considerable dangers to your boy from this misapprehension, not to mention the possibility of an embarrassing misunderstanding between himself and members of the female sex. Would it be possible for you and his mother to have a talk with him and improve the worst areas of his ignorance?

    I am very worried about his being in contact with girl students until he has got his mind sorted out.

Yours sincerely,

A. Caballeros, B.A.
Senior Science Master

P.S.   When you have sorted him out on the female side, you might try to do the same on the male. Please convince him the male organ is not shaped like a bowl of fruit and is not situated in the neck.

Wragby Hall,
Notts.
Sept. 4, 1921

Dear Mellors,

I regret that I must give you notice to leave my employment at the end of the week. You have been guilty of scandalous conduct; you have deceived me; you have committed a terrible breach of the trust I reposed in you by utterly neglecting your duties as gamekeeper over the last six months.

As you know, I had one hundred and twenty guests down for a shoot on September 1st. The guests included such distinguished persons as the President of the Mineowners' Association and his lady wife and the general who commanded my old division in France just before I was wounded so severely. You may imagine my feelings when you were able to put up only three birds and one of those had only got one leg. These three birds were immediately blown to pieces by the concentrated fire of 120 shotguns, leaving the guests with nothing to do for the rest of the week. Some were so frustrated they were reduced to shooting sparrows and wood pigeons, while others shot the beaters and one actually shot at me.

Your explanation, "Tha must ask Connie, happen she can explain what Ah've been doing," was absolute rubbish, as you must realise. I cannot see what Lady Chatterley has to do with it. As you know, most of my guests left next day in disgust.

The fact is, Mellors, that almost all of the birds had been killed when young by predators such as foxes, due to your neglect. You never seem to be about the place these days but always in your cottage with the blinds drawn. I have hardly seen you around the estate for four months. When you do make an appearance you seem worn-out and haggard. Your manner appears strange and preoccupied. What were you doing with those flowers in your hair the other day? Is anything wrong? However, that is your business. You must leave my employ but in case you are in any domestic difficulty I will send Lady Chatterley down to visit you before then and see if there is anything you want.

Yours, etc.

Sir Clifford Chatterley

Dearest Brother,

Our fortunes are made! I have taken the money
which father left us in his will and have invested it in
the surest and safest commodity, none other than
that herb which both refreshes and stimulates. I
need hardly say I am referring to the fragrant
infusion which delights our mornings and
rejuvenates our afternoons, viz. TEA.

I have laid out the whole of our legacy with a
merchant in the City of London, here in Mincing
Lane, and with it he has purchased a 64th share in
the voyage of the good ship *Susan*, a stoutly-built
barque of some 500 tons, at present loading near
London Bridge. She is taking on a cargo of tea, and
this will fetch five times its price when it is
eventually sold abroad. I have spoken to her captain
who assures me that he himself bought a 32nd share
of her last voyage and made a profit well in excess of
£9,000, sufficient to enable him to retire after this
next voyage to a country house and a four-in-hand.
The mate of the ship says all on board are so
prosperous that the men think nothing of giving
their doxies gold watches, while silk scarves and
stockings for the wharfside drabs are as common as
string.

This, then, is the happy commerce to which I have
entrusted all our money. I need hardly say the
owners of the vessel are as sanguine as the captain,
nay, more so, since they have reaped an even bigger
fortune.

The ship sails next Thursday and I shall be there
to wish her godspeed. But stay! I have not told you
where she is to travel to gain all this fortune that

surely awaits her. The owner, whom I met in Lloyd's coffee house, tells me that the surest place for a good profit on her cargo is the American colonies, where the demand for tea is insatiable, despite the new tax. She should reach there within two months and by Christmas her cargo will be sold at an enormous profit on the quayside at Boston, one of the principal ports of that country. Boston! I fear it will not be anything like our own fair Lincolnshire city, doubtless being full of rude savages, but even colonials are not entirely devoid of civilised taste and unless they throw the cargo into the sea, we are both surely rich men!

Your loving brother,

John

My Dear Sigmund,

I cannot tell you how much sorrow you are bringing to your dear Mother's heart with this foolish branch of science you have descended to. This new book of yours disgusted me and brought disgrace to the Freud family. How could you bring yourself to say those awful things about mothers and tell those poor sick people that their parents were to blame for their madness?

Believe me, I always tried to be a good mother to you. When you were a tiny baby I refused to breast feed you in case you caught germs. And I did not make the mistake of spoiling you. I beat you every day to ensure you understood discipline and you appreciated that. I also allowed you to sleep with your father and myself in our bed, even at our most intimate moments, because you wanted to come in with us. As you got older I woke you up every two hours at night to stop evil dreams. I even dressed you in your sister's old clothes until you were ten, to save money.

And what thanks did we get? As soon as you could toddle you went around trying to stab your father and make love to your sister and me. We tried everything—bromide in your coffee, cold baths, long walks—but all to no avail. However, as you got older you settled down and we began to hope that at long last all the careful devotion we had exercised was about to be rewarded. When you entered medical school we were so proud and the finest day of our lives was when you graduated, even though you spoiled everything that day by another attempt to knife Papa.

And now all our hopes are dashed. You have

invented these wild theories about mothers being to blame for everything and published them, together with disgusting details of other people's private thoughts and lives. The neighbours will no longer talk to us, and I do not blame them. I can see them looking at me in the street and thinking, "How could she have brought him up so badly?" Your poor Papa is grief-stricken and the knife scars on his back hurt him so badly in the cold weather.

As for your sister, you have destroyed any chance she ever had of getting married. Who would want a girl whose brother writes about boys wanting to make love to their sisters and mothers? Oh, the shame of it!

Please, Sigmund, for our sakes give it up.

Your loving mother

P.S.   Be sure to wear your warm socks this weather and to beat yourself every day. If you cannot beat yourself get somebody else to do it.

14, rue Noire,
Paris

To The Emperor Napoleon   Jan. 5, 1809

Sire,

    As one who is deeply honoured to be your
personal tailor may I humbly venture to make two
suggestions that will make Your Imperial Highness
an even more majestic and awe-inspiring figure on
your public appearances.

    Firstly, I would humbly request that instead of
always sticking your right hand into the left side of
your waistcoat, you could sometimes use the left
hand thrust into the right side? This will even out
the wear on the waistcoats and they will last longer,
as at present the left side gets a hole in it very
quickly. Also it gets out of shape.

    Secondly, I wonder if I could persuade Your
Highness not to wear your hat sideways? They are
meant to be worn so they stick out in front and
behind, not jutting out beyond the ears. If you look
at the way The Duke of Wellington wears his hat
next time you are in battle, you will see what I mean.
I hope Your Highness will not be offended at my
presumption in offering this advice but the whole
French people have followed your example with the
result we are the only nation in Europe that wears its
hats sideways.

    I am only thinking of Your Highness's reputation.
It would be terrible if you were to be remembered
not as the saviour of Europe but as the man who
always stuck his hand in his waistcoat and wore his
hats crosswise.

                    Your loyal subject,

                    Jean-Baptiste Brun
                    Imperial Tailor

72

CHAPMAN AND HALL, PUBLISHERS

31, Holborn,
London
June 5, 1870

Dear Mr. Dickens,

What on earth is happening over *Edwin Drood*?
You have so far sent us no fewer than 36 possible
endings, all of them totally unsuitable. We do not
think it a good idea for the murderer to turn out to
be Carker, resurrected from *Dombey and Son* with
the remark, "Yes, it is I, Carker, I was not killed by
the railway train after all." Nor do we think suicide
is a good solution. Your latest suggestion, received
yesterday, is absolutely ridiculous. It is extremely
contrived for the whole town to burst into flames,
destroying all the characters, and as you put it, "thus
removing for ever all evidence as to who killed
Edwin Drood," although we appreciate this ending
would save you a lot of trouble.

I know you have been in bad health recently, but I
really must insist you get down to the job and finish
this book at once as the printers are waiting.

Yours sincerely,

F. Chapman

July 3, 1026

Canute,
King of Mercia, Wessex and Anglia

My Liege,
    High tide at Chichester on July 6 is at 10.07 a.m.

Your servant,

Olfric

Dear Madam,

I cannot tell you how sorry I am about the
accident to your son yesterday.

What happened was that I looked out as usual on
the feast of Stephen, when the snow lay round about,
deep and crisp and even. Brightly shone the moon
that night, though the frost was cruel, and I noticed
an old peasant blundering about in the snow
gathering winter fuel. Feeling sorry for him, I called
your son, who was on duty as page that evening, to
accompany me and together we sallied forth to invite
the peasant to dine at the Palace as my guest.
Unfortunately, your son, who is not very tall, found
difficulty in walking through the snow and said in a
shrill voice (F sharp) that he could go no further. I
then suggested he should put his feet in my
footsteps. He did this, and made good progress by
treading in the very sod that I had printed.

Now the peasant lived a good league hence,
underneath the mountain, over by the forest fence,
by St. Agnes Fountain, and to reach the cottage one
had to cross a ravine. On reaching this, I turned
sharply to walk along the edge to a bridge, but alas
your son, following my footsteps blindly with his
head down, walked straight over the edge and fell 20
feet into the deep snow at the bottom.

It took two hours to dig him out but the doctor
says he will be all right in about a week if
complications don't set in.

Please accept my deepest apologies. I shall bring
him home personally when the weather moderates.

Yours sincerely,

Wenceslaus

Florence
Jan. 9, 1493

Dear Lucretia,

Just a quick note to thank you so much for the lovely dinner party last night. The food was absolutely delicious and that special dish you prepared for Rudolpho really appealed to him, with its peculiar sharp taste. Talking of Rudolpho, a strange thing happened after we got home. His face turned black and a jet of steam shot out of his ears and whenever he breathed on anything it caught fire. Fortunately he is now sleeping soundly, in fact he has slept for 12 hours and cannot be woken, no matter how much we bang the door. Still, the rest will do him good.

With love,

Maria

31, Main Street,
Centerville,
Kentucky,
U.S.A.
April 23, 1879

Dear Mr. Edison,
    Along with this letter I am enclosing one of your new incandescent electric illumination globes, with the request that you will repair or replace it, as it appears to be faulty. There seems to be no hole at which to light it. I have struck a whole box of matches, but it will just not take fire. Also, there seems no place to adjust the wick. I wonder if the supply line is too small for the fuel to pass through.
    Incidentally, what is that screw near the door for?

Yours, etc.

J. Daniel Jackson

From: Lord Raglan, C-in-C British Army in the Crimea

To: Lord Cardigan, Commanding the Light Brigade of Cavalry

Dear Lord Cardigan,

Thank you very much for the instructions on how to knit one of these little woollen jackets you wear so stylishly, which have arrived via your valet.
However, I am having some slight difficulty. I am all right knitting the bodywork, but the sleeves are proving troublesome. I am not very good at turning and I can't decrease for the life of me. Also is "K1, P1, K2 tog." correct? Could your valet have made a mistake? I made an effort at the sleeves but only succeeded in closing up the armholes so that can't be right.

I wonder if it is the needles? I am using old musket cleaning-rods at present and perhaps these are not suitable. My own valet cannot help as he is a buffoon from the Argyll and Sutherland Highlanders and his knowledge of knitting is limited, to say the least.

Please forgive my sending this note to you in the middle of the battle, but it is rather important and there is a lull at present. I am sending it by my trusted aide, Capt. Nolan, and I would be grateful for a quick reply, but be sure to write your instructions down and not trust to the spoken word. Capt. Nolan is an excellent soldier but rather inclined to be hot-headed and to mis-interpret instructions.

Raglan

The President of the Tribunal,
Paris

Sir,
   Fool! Imbecile! Pig! Name of a dog! You are
using my wonderful new invention all wrong! You
are supposed to execute people kneeling down, not
standing up. If you execute aristocrats standing up,
you will need 100 graves for fifty aristocrats, as they
will all be split down the middle.
   Also, Monsieur, the baskets in front of the
machines are for holding heads, not balls of wool.
   If you would like me to, I shall be happy to give
you a personal demonstration of how the new
machine should work.

My distinguished sentiments,

Jacques Guillotine (Dr.)

Dear Isabella,

Just a line to say I had a most wonderful welcome from the lads when I arrived here yesterday. They greeted me with ten thousand armed men all shouting and waving their weapons and escorted me to this lovely little island in the Thames. Now Isabella dear, don't worry, but I may be just a little bit delayed in my return. It's so nice here that the boys have persuaded me to stay a little longer and have a quiet chat about one or two matters. It might be a good idea, sweetheart, if you didn't leave the castle for the next few days, huh? I'd like you to be home in any case to look after my bodyguard, who will be returning by themselves tomorrow. The boys felt their presence spoiled the harmony of the occasion and of course I agreed with them.

All here are in good health, although Hubert de Burgh has a touch of ague. Simon de Montfort and Steve Langton send their best wishes. Must hurry along now, as a messenger has arrived to say the lads are anxious for me to join them and they don't like to be kept waiting.

Home soon, I hope.

Your loving husband,

John

Dear Mr. Shaw,

I wonder if you have any old manuscripts that we could knock into shape as a film? I looked at a play of yours called *The Doctor's Dilemma* once and it was just great only we would have to change it somewhat since the hero is diseased and the public don't like films about disease which is why La Bohème has never been seen on the screen. Also your hero dies and we would have to alter it so he lived. And all your villains are doctors. We find the public don't like doctors to be villains as it upsets their sense of security so they would have to be good men, too. Perhaps you could make the villains all politicians. We find crooked politicians go down well.

Looking forward to hearing from you.

Sam Goldwyn

19, rue des Capucines
Paris
March 5, 1895

Dear Mr. Van Gogh,

I cannot tell you how distressed I am about what happened this morning. Such a thing has not happened in all my thirty years in the business. Believe me, it was not my fault. It was all caused by that sudden loud noise in the street outside that caused me to swing round while shaving you.

I sincerely hope you make a speedy recovery and that this unfortunate mischance will not stop you from patronising my barber's shop. I also hope that you will still be able to go ahead with the self-portrait you were working on. Perhaps you could paint out the left ear?

I shall visit you in hospital as soon as time permits. Believe me, if ever you want a free shave you shall have it on demand.

Yours sincerely,

Antoine

The Surgery,
Dunsinane
Friday

Your Majesty,
    I have examined the Queen again, and I now
believe her depression and sleepwalking are largely
due to indigestion. I think she has been forcing
herself to attend too many banquets. You may
remember the illness first showed itself after the
great celebration in honour of the late and lamented
Lord Banquo. In this connection, the morbid fear of
blood which she shows is possibly a symptom of
revulsion at too much tomato soup.
    I hope Her Majesty will recover and soon be fit to
take her usual walk in Birnam Wood. Apropos of
Birnam Wood, I should inform Your Majesty a large
group of roughly-dressed men appeared yesterday
and carried most of it away on their backs. I trust
they had permission.
    I take the liberty of enclosing my reckoning for
attendance since the start of Your Majesty's reign.

ITEM	To attendance on bleeding sergeant	1s.	$4\frac{3}{4}$d.
ITEM	To attendance on the late King Duncan, applying tourniquets, etc.	3s.	5d.
ITEM	The same to King Duncan's two grooms	2s.	6d.
ITEM	To setting leg of drunken porter after he fell downstairs	0s.	1d.
ITEM	Post mortem on Lord Banquo	0s.	7d.

ITEM	To attendance on Queen on various occasions during illness at Glamis, Dunsinane and elsewhere	5£	6s.	8¾d.
ITEM	To night calls to Queen	10£	3s.	4½d.
ITEM	Hire of gentlewoman as night nurse	1£	2s.	5d.
ITEM	Sleeping draughts	3£	11s.	6d.
ITEM	Arabian perfumes		1s.	4d.

I have the honour to be sire,
Your obedient servant

J. Macdonald,
Physician to the King

BEFORE

AFTER

University of Yale
July 4, 1920

Prof. Rutherford,
Cavendish Laboratory,
Cambridge University,
Cambridge

Dear Professor Rutherford,
    About that formula of mine, $E = MC^2$. I'm sorry to tell you I made a mistake. It is wrong. It should be $E = R^3 + \frac{2}{5}(x^2 - y) + 1$.
    If you use the old formula it blows up. I know. I tried it.
    Sorry about this. Hope you haven't used too much time on the research.

        Sincerely,

        Albert Einstein

Boston,
Mass.
Oct. 5, 1898

Dear Jack,

Well, it is all over now and I am gradually getting used to the fame that attaches itself to a man who has just become the first to sail round the world in a small boat. It seems a long time since I set out from Boston in *The Spray* and now time is hanging heavy on my hands and I intend to write the story of the voyage. However, before I do, I have a confession to make. The fact is, Jack, I did not sail round the world. Oh yes, I made a long voyage all right, and I guess I sailed mostways round the world, but to tell the truth I cut a corner. Quite a considerable corner in fact, no less than the entire sub-continent of South America.

Now you will immediately ask, as a seaman yourself, how anyone could miss passing Cape Horn in a round-the-world voyage, and I will tell you.

I went overland.

The trouble was that I kept hitting South America every time I tried to go round Cape Horn. A lot of people say I am an expert in navigation. Actually that's all my eye. All I had to navigate by was a compass and an old alarm clock which is why I went to Gibraltar first from Boston. I was aiming to go south but somehow I kept going east. And then I turned and headed for where I thought Cape Horn was but I kept running into Brazil. In the end a storm forced me north and I had to beach *The Spray* and found myself on the Isthmus of Panama. I then realised the Pacific Ocean was only 40 miles away across the narrow strip of land and I thought, why bother to sail 5,000 miles round Cape Horn to reach the Pacific if I could carry *The Spray* 40 miles?

My mind was made up by the appearance of a tribe of Indians, who made friends with me. By signs I indicated my intention and they agreed to help upon promise of some pieces of mirror and a few nails. I'd built *The Spray* myself so I knew every inch of her and it wasn't difficult to dismantle the boat and give the pieces to the Indians to carry across the swamp and jungle to the Pacific, a task they accomplished in a fortnight.

Once on the other shore I bade my rude friends farewell and started to rebuild the boat with the aid of four or five Indians who stayed to assist me.

I had intended to make public my adventure, but on reaching Australia I was hailed with such enthusiasm for my feat of navigation and seamanship that I had not the heart to tell the truth. It is difficult to admit to a lie when the band is playing *See the Conquering Hero Comes*, and I guess I succumbed to human weakness.

So there you are, Jack. You are the only one who knows my secret and I know you will never confide it to another human soul.

Your friend,

Josh Slocum

299858 PO WD G

TW TRC TELEGRAM G

051448

ZCZC TXB0561 BSC 959 Z195 LUCKLON

GBXX CO GBBS 010

MONMOUTH 10 5 1104

LUCKY ESTRAGON

PSOPHIDIAN

LONDON W1

CALLED BUT YOU WERE OUT

GODOT

COL ESTRAGON PSOPHIDIAN LONDONW1

NNNN

299858 PO WD G

TW TRC TELEGRAM G

Thursday

To: General J. Custer
Commanding 7th Cavalry U.S. Army

Sir,
    I have the honour to report that in accordance with your instructions I have thoroughly scouted the area around Little Big Horn and beg to report there be no signs of any Indians.

J. Adams (Lieut.)

From: Napoleon Bonaparte, Emperor
of the French; First Consul for
Life; First Citizen of France; King
in absentia of the United Kingdom
of Great Britain and Ireland;
Commander-in-Chief of the Imperial
Grand Army of France; Commander
of the First Military District;
Commander of the Second Military
District; Commander of the Third
Military District; Colonel-in-Chief
of the Old Guard; Head of the
Deuxième Bureau; Controller of the
Troisième Bureau; Commander of
the Légion d'Honneur; Chief of the
Imperial Order of St. Anthony;
holder of the Médaille Militaire with
oak leaves; holder of the award for
meritorious service (with branches).

To: The Empress Josephine of all
France; Queen *in absentia* of the
United Kingdom of Great Britain
and Ireland; Grand Dame of the
Imperial Order of St. Anthony.

Leipzig, Friday

Madam,

It has been reported to me by those whom I
employ to furnish me with information on these
matters that on the past three days a pair of men's
boots has been found under your bed.

I desire your explanation of this immediately.

I need hardly remind you that the Emperor's wife
must be above suspicion.

Bonaparte

From: The Empress Josephine of all France, Queen *in absentia* of the United Kingdom of Great Britain and Ireland; Grand Dame of the Imperial Order of St. Anthony.

To: Napoleon Bonaparte, Emperor of the French; First Consul for Life; First Citizen of France; King *in absentia* of the United Kingdom of Great Britain and Ireland; Commander-in-Chief of the Imperial Grand Army of France; Commander of the First Military District; Commander of the Second Military District; Commander of the Third Military District; Colonel-in-Chief of the Old Guard; Head of the Deuxième Bureau; Controller of the Troisième Bureau; Commander of the Légion d'Honneur; Chief of the Imperial Order of St. Anthony; holder of the Médaille Militaire with oak leaves; holder of the award for meritorious service (with branches).

Paris, Thursday

It's all right, Boney. They were only Wellingtons.

Josephine